A BOOK FOR GIRLS ABOUT BEING A GIRL!

By Penelope Dyan

Table of Poems

1. **ABOUT GIRLS**

2. **SUGER AND SPICE**

3. **COOKING**

4. **ON BEING A GIRL**

5. **BAD HAIR DAY**

6. **ON NOSES**

7. **ON GOING TO THE POTTY**

8. **MY DOLLY**

9. **WHEN I GROW UP**

10. **ABOUT MY HAIR**

11. **THE MUD COOKIE**

12. **SOMETHING I HATE**

13. **WHAT MOM SAYS**

14. **LIPSTICK**

15. **WHY**

16. CINDERELLA

17. WHEN I GROW UP

18. MICKEY BITES

19. THE PIG GOT OUT!

20. BEAUTY PARLOR

21. ADVICE ON SHOES

22. TAPPING

23. OTHER STUFF AND ABOUT MY BROTHER

24. THE BOY AT SCHOOL

25. ON BEING A BEAUTY QUEEN

26. ABOUT BATHS AND DUCKS

27. BOO BOOS

28. WHY I LIKE TO DANCE

29. MY BIG HAIR

30. MY PRAYER

31. BUBBLE BATHS

32. MY BARBIE

33. ABOUT RUNNING

34. I HATE BUGS!

35. WHAT I REALLY LIKE

36. MY BROTHER'S ROOM

37. SISTERS

38. SWEET STUFF

39. BAD WORDS

40. ON BEING GOOD

41. OUR KITTY

42. A WISH

43. ON MOPPING THE FLOOR

44. ABOUT THE SKY

45. ADDING TO THE FAMILY

46. BOYS

47. GOING TO THE MALL

48. MY GARDEN

49. THINGS I HAVE AND THINGS I LIKE

50. THE TEACHER'S PET

51. TEARS

52. MY CAT

53. MY DOG

54. THE HOLES IN MY EARS

55. THE GOOD NIGHT

56. TEA WITH DOLLY

57. DUST BUNNIES

58. RUFFLEY SOCKS

59. BOYS STINK

60. PETER PAN

61. ABOUT MONEY

62. MY MOM SAYS

63. BEES

64. THE END

Forward

Hey Girls, this book is just for you,
For all the silly things you say and do.
I know your tricks because you see,
You're all girls, just like me!
And when all is said and done,
Girls are just girls and girls have fun!
So boys go away and do your own thing
And leave us alone to dance and sing!

A Book For Girls About Being A Girl

ABOUT GIRLS

Girls are special,
Girls are sweet,
Girls never have smelly feet.

When Girls sweat
They only glow,
Ask any girl.
She ought to know.

Girls, if they had their druthers.
Would have only sisters
And no brothers.

Boys smell and spit
And they make poo,
And this is something,
Girls just don't do.

A Book For Girls About Being A Girl

SUGAR AND SPICE

**It's true that girls are all sugar and spice,
And they only do things that are very nice,
Except when they get tangled hair,
And then they're bad
Because they swear!**

A Book For Girls About Being A Girl

COOKING

**If you want to take a look,
You can see my sisters cook.
There's floor dust everywhere,
On the floor and in their hair.
But when they're done it's really funny
'Cause what they've made
Tastes really yummy!**

A Book For Girls About Being A Girl

ON BEING A GIRL

If you're a girl
You can do anything,
If you believe you can.
You can be anyone
You want to be,
You don't have to be a man.
You can be a doctor, a lawyer,
You can sing,
You can do just anything.
You can be a Mommy,
Yes you can
And you can't do that
If you're a man!

A Book For Girls About Being A Girl

BAD HAIR DAY

I hate having a bad hair day,
And then I just wish it would go away.
The alternative would be to have no hair,
I'd wear a hat, I wouldn't care.
I'd wear a hat with a great big feather,
Except when there was rainy weather.
Because then I'd have a bad feather day,
And want the hat to go away.

A Book For Girls About Being A Girl

ON NOSES

**Girls are always good
And never cranky;
They blow their nose
Into a hanky.**

**They never, ever pick their nose,
Because as to burghers,
They have none of those.**

A Book For Girls About Being A Girl

ON GOING TO THE POTTY

When girls pee,
They never miss the pot,
Because they sit down to go
And they do it a lot.
But as to boys it isn't fair,
Because they can pee just anywhere,
In a field, or from a tree,
Like rain it comes down,
But it's just pee.
And another thing that isn't fair,
They don't pull down their underwear,
Except when they go number two,
Then they sit on the pot,
Yes they do!

A Book For Girls About Being A Girl

MY DOLLY

I like to put my dolly to bed:
I cover her up, right up to her head,
And then I give her a good night kiss,
Because I just like doing this.

My dolly isn't real and I know that's true,
But it's just for practice and for something to do!

It's quiet and comforting and between you and me,
I'm practicing for what someday I will be.

I'll be a mommy just like you!
With ever so much I'll have to do.
But at night when my baby must go right to bed,
I'll give her a kiss and not cover her head!

A Book For Girls About Being A Girl

WHEN I GROW UP

When I grow up
I'll be just like my mother,
I wear high heeled shoes
And something or other.
And I just know I'll have to dye my hair,
And I'll be so beautiful
They'll just have to stare!
Maybe I'll add
A false eyelash or two,
I want to be just like you!
I'll put some powder and lipstick on my face,
And spray the perfume just every place,
And when I go out,
I'll wear my very best dress,
And leave the house a great big mess!

A Book For Girls About Being A Girl

ABOUT MY HAIR

When I dance I jump into the air,
Not even thinking about my hair
As I leap to who knows where
My hair just goes everywhere!

Sometimes it lands right in my face
It never seems to stay in place
Why do I have so much hair?
That sticks out here and sticks out there?

If I took a scissors
I could take care of it,
But then my mom would have a fit.
She'd say, "Where is all your beautiful hair?"
And I'd point to the trashcan over there!

And then I think she'd probably die;
In the very least she'd start to cry!
Because she just *loves* my beautiful hair
Messy and just everywhere.

A Book For Girls About Being A Girl

THE MUD COOKIE

Once I baked a big mud cookie
It was big and oh so ooky!
My fingernails filled with dirt
When mom scrubbed them
It kind of hurt.

I got some mud in my hair,
In fact I got it everywhere.
Then mommy put me in the tub
And I really had to scrub
Until at last I was so clean
I looked just like a beauty queen!

A Book For Girls About Being A Girl

SOMETHING I HATE

Boys look up my dress
So I wear shorts under there;
Otherwise they'd look and see
My polka dotted underwear.

Then I can climb the monkey bars
Or I can climb a tree
Because then when the boys look up
A pair of shorts they see.

Why they even want to look
I'll never, ever know,
If asked to take a peek at theirs?
I'd shout a great big "NO!"

A Book For Girls About Being A Girl

WHAT MOM SAYS

My Mom is very smart,
She says getting men to do what you want
Is really an art.

She says you can get them to do anything,
They will jump over a fence or
They'll even sing.

She says you use something
Called the feminine wile
And how you use it is a matter of style.

She says you should use everything
That you have got and that you
Should use it a lot.

My mom believes in the feminist life,
But she says to use everything
Once you're a wife.

I don't understand what she's trying to say,
But she says I'll understand when
I need it someday.

A Book For Girls About Being A Girl

LIPSTICK

I like to put lipstick on my face
Even if it gets all over the place,
I like to wear a long string of pearl,
Because after all, I am a girl.

I like to wear Mom's best dress
And her best shoes and make a mess.
I like to primp and powder and fluff,
Until I'm done and had enough..

And then I'll put it all away
And go downstairs and start to play
Mom sees my face and then I'll grin
Because it's her makeup I've been in.

"I told you to stay out of my stuff!"
Says my Mom, "I've had enough!"
So I look at her and start to cry
As a plop of glob falls in my eye.

"I won't do it again," I sincerely say;
She washes my face, I go out and play.
I guess I'm just practicing, you see,
For when I grow up and who I will be!

A Book For Girls About Being A Girl

WHY

Why are girls different than boys?
And why do we like different toys?
Mom says we're different inside and out,
And girls are quiet and boys just shout.
But I don't think that this is true
Because sometimes shout is what I do!
Especially of my brother gets under my skin
Then I just want to get rid of him.
And so I shout, "Get out of my hair!"
"And stop looking at my underwear!"
"And turn around and get out of my room!"
"You better do it and do it soon!"
And then he whines to Mommy just like a baby
Because unlike me, he's not a lady!

CINDERELLA

Someday I'll be
Just like Cinderella
And live in a castle
With Prince Charming,
My fella.
I'll have lots of mice
That I'll dress up in clothes;
And I'll dance at the ball
Because everyone knows
That this is how a fairytale goes!
Mommy says fairytales can come true,
Because Dad's been her prince
Since they said, "I do!
Even if he snores
And sometimes he'll spit,
Mommy doesn't mind it,
Not once single bit.

A Book For Girls About Being A Girl

WHEN I GROW UP

When I grow up
I'll be who I will be
Whether it's skinny or it's fat.
I will be who I will be
And that will just be that!

I'll be happy
With who I will be,
Whether I'm skinny or I'm fat'
Because it's what's inside of me
That matters and that's that!

A Book For Girls About Being A Girl

MICKEY BITES

**It was dark in the house
I got a night light, Mickey Mouse.**

**"Now you won't be afraid," Dad said,
When you climb at night into your bed.**

**"Don't touch that light," my mommy said,
As she kissed me on my head.**

**Then one night I poked at it,
And I found out that Mickey bit!**

A Book For Girls About Being A Girl

THE PIG GOT OUT!

One day the pig got out,
And my mom began in fear to shout.
At that time I had just turned three,
And the pig was huge
Much bigger than me!,
And so I called, "Here piggy, piggy, piggy,"
As mom stood by in fear,
And then the pig followed me into his pen,
Just like a little dear!
I'm just glad it wasn't the duck,
'Cause then she'd just be out of luck,

A Book For Girls About Being A Girl

BEAUTY PARLOR

If you decide to play beauty parlor,
Don't *ever* cut off your hair!
Because your mom might shout at you,
And she *migh*t even swear.

A Book For Girls About Being A Girl

ADVICE ON SHOES

**Speaking of shoes,
A girl needs a lot,
So count how many you have got.**

**Shoes must match the dress you wear
They are just as important
As the bows in your hair,**

**Keep a penny in your shoe,
For luck and a gum ball
One will do.**

**If you put in more it won't feel right,
And your shoe
Becomes too tight.**

**Your mom will take you to the store
Because she thinks
That you need more.**

**When they take off your shoe after you limp
Through the door
And fifty pennies fall to the floor . . ,**

**Everyone will have a laughing fit,
And you'll never hear
The end of it!**

A Book For Girls About Being A Girl

TAPPING

I like my taps shoes,
They make lots of noise,
I shuffle and turn,
And dance with some boys.
Shuffle hop
Shuffle step
Shuffle hop shuffle scuff.
These boys are dumb,
And I've had enough!
All they do is stop and stare!
They probably want to see
My underwear!

A Book For Girls About Being A Girl

OTHER STUFF AND ABOUT MY BROTHER

Mommy brushes my hair
One hundred strokes a night
And if I don't get my beauty sleep
She says I'll look a fright.

I keep my bedroom
Cozy and neat,
Because I'm a girl
And I am sweet!

I never fight with my brother
He just fights with me over
Something or other,

Because I am perfect
Don't you see?
I'm just as perfect
As I can be!

But though I'm perfect
If you ask my mother
She'll tell you that I fight
With my brother,

And not that he
Just fights with me,
And that I am as perfect
As can be!

She says sometimes
I just start a fight
And that it
Isn't ever right!

A Book For Girls About Being A Girl

THE BOY AT SCHOOL

There is a boy at school
Who thinks that I am really cool,
He says I'm a girl like no other,
But he only reminds me of my brother!

A Book For Girls About Being A Girl

ON BEING A BEAUTY QUEEN

I like to dance and I like to sing
I want to be a beauty queen!
I want to walk right down the ramp
And smile and look just like a vamp!
And when they say I've won the crown,
And the other girls begin to frown.
I'll smile and wave and know I'm the best;
But if I lose, you can imagine the rest!
I might even throw a fit!
And then that will be the end of it!
I'll just never be a beauty queen,
And all because I made a scene!

A Book For Girls About Being A Girl

ABOUT BATHS AND DUCKS

I like lots of bubbles in my tub,
And I play and primp while I scrub.
I have a little rubber ducky,
That turned black inside and really yucky,
Then I found I was in luck,
When mom bought me a brand new duck!
Now I play rub a dub ducky,
In my tub cause he's not yucky!
And ducky watches me wash my hair,
With bubbles, bubbles everywhere!

A Book For Girls About Being A Girl

BOO BOOS

When I fall down and skin my knee,
My mom comes out to rescue me.
She cleans the boo-boo nice and clean
Around the edge and in between.
She seals it with a bandage and a kiss;
When I grow up I'll sure miss this.
Then when I trip and fall,
My mommy won't come out at all!
I love my mommy, yes I do,
She will even rescue you!

A Book For Girls About Being A Girl

WHY I LIKE TO DANCE

I like to cartwheel and handspring
And twirl and dance and spin.
I dance because I am happy
And happy's the mood that I'm in!

A Book For Girls About Being A Girl

MY BIG HAIR

My hair is curly all over the place,
It goes down my back and hangs over my face.

I could look just like a ball of hair
And run around just everywhere

Then Mom would ask, "Where is Sue?"
"There's something that I want to do."

"I want to take her shopping today,
But apparently she's run away."

"I was going to the ice-cream store
To get a cone, and maybe more."

Then I would appear from under my hair,
I would come out from under there.

And we would go to the store,
To buy some ice-cream and maybe more,

A Book For Girls About Being A Girl

MY PRAYER

I prayed to God tonight
Before I went to bed
I prayed my bother wouldn't beat me up
'Cause I hit him on the head.
And because he's bigger than me
I'll hide behind my mother's knee
And then in a day or two or three
He'll forget that it was me
Who smacked him there upon his head
Just before we went to bed.

A Book For Girls About Being A Girl

TEASING

I'm a tease and I tease a bit,
I just can't stop dong it.
It's like dancing and singing
It's part of me
I've been a tease since I was three.
My mother says, "Don't tease your brother,"
Go outside and so something or other,
Then I go outside and play
Back to tease another day.

A Book For Girls About Being A Girl

BUBBLE BATHS

I don't like to take a shower
Because bubble baths give me power
I like to just sit and soak
And take my time and that's no joke.
Sometimes I even like to sing,
And I blow bubbles in between.
My cat sits right next to my tub;
He watches me and sees me scrub.
And then I put some bubbles on his hair
And he runs around just everywhere!
And then I just laugh aloud with glee
'Cause he's as funny as can be.
A bath can be a real delight,
When you bathe and do it right!

A Book For Girls About Being A Girl

MY BARBIE

I had a Barbie,
I bit off her toes,
I put nail polish on her nose.
Then I cut off all of her hair,
Lost her clothes,
She had nothing to wear.

My brother said,
"She's still a fox;
She doesn't need
Her long blond locks!"
I put her down into
My drawer
I hoped to see her
Nevermore!

A Book For Girls About Being A Girl

ABOUT RUNNING

When I go outside I like to run,
Through the grass and in the sun;
When I run I haven't a care,
I like to feel the cool crisp air!
And when I run in the fall,
I like the leaves most of all
I like to squash them under my feet
The crunching sound is really neat.

A Book For Girls About Being A Girl

I HATE BUGS!

**I hate spiders, can't stand a fly;
If you ask I'll tell you why!**

**Spiders, spiders everywhere
Sticky webs stick in my hair!**

**I can't even climb a tree
Without a fly biting me.**

**And if I ever see an ant
I run away and start to rant,**

**Sometimes Il look under my rug
And there I find an ugly bug.**

**I think my brother puts it there,
Just to try to give a scare!**

A Book For Girls About Being A Girl

WHAT I REALLY LIKE

I love roses, candy too,
I'm just a little girl like you!
I love dollies, and I love dresses,
I like having beautiful tresses!
I like wearing fancy clothes,
I like powder on my nose!
I like flowers in my hair,
I like when people stop and stare.
And most of all besides my kitty,
I like looking oh so pretty!

A Book For Girls About Being A Girl

MY BROTHER'S ROOM

Sometimes I hear a great big boom!
It comes right from my bother's room.
My friend looks at me and then I say,
"Never mind, it's just his way!"
Then I hear my mother shout,
"Stop that noise and just go out!"
He just threw something to make a noise,
That's how it is with little boys!

A Book For Girls About Being A Girl

SISTERS

**When it comes to sisters my brother has three,
And one of them is little me!
We try to just stay put of his way,
But then he comes and wants to play.
Pretty soon things get rough,
And he screams for Mommy
He's not so tough!**

A Book For Girls About Being A Girl

SWEET STUFF

One thing that is a riot
Is when my mommy's on a diet.
She tries to watch what she eats
And stays away from all those sweets.
But here's one thing that's just not fair,
Then we can't eat them! We don't dare!

We like ice-cream and candy too!
But she's on a diet, so what can we do?
She says we need good eating rules,
They teach that in all the schools;
But sometimes we just like a treat,
Something chewy, thick and sweet!

A Book For Girls About Being A Girl

BAD WORDS

Sometimes my brother says a bad word,
Something that I've never heard!
He tells me not to tell our mummy,
Or he'll punch me in my tummy.
But to mummy I will run,
Spoiling all his bad boy fun.
Then she sends him to his room.
Where he sings another tune.
He doesn't punch me in my tummy
"Cause I will only run to mummy.

A Book For Girls About Being A Girl

ON BEING GOOD

Us girls are better than our brother,
Just you go and ask our mother!
We hardly ever misbehave,
Or we'd send mummy to her grave!
Sometimes, though, we kids all fight,
Even though it isn't right.
But we girls never shout or swear,
And we change our underwear!

A Book For Girls About Being A Girl

OUR KITTY

Sometimes kitty gets a hairball,
He scratches the furniture and that's not all!
Sometimes he catches a little mouse,
And brings it into mommy's house.
Then mommy says, "Get rid of it!"
If no one does, she has a fit.
When our kitty becomes a cat,
I'll bet he catches a great big rat!
Then our mommy will really scream,
And think she's in a real bad dream!

A Book For Girls About Being A Girl

A WISH

**I wish I had a feather bed,
And there I'd lay my little head.**

**I'd like my bed up in a tree,
Then no one near could bother me.**

**There in the tree the birds would sing.
'til they flew off on bended wing.**

**The butterflies would flitter and fly,
And I'd look up at the clear blue sky!**

ON MOPPING THE FLOOR

Sometimes I like to mop the floor
Mom says I make a mess,
Then I take a look around
And she's right, I guess!

A Book For Girls About Being A Girl

ABOUT THE SKY

How high is the sky I wonder?
And from where comes all the thunder?
Is God beating his drum on high
Way beyond the great blue sky?

And why does the sky turn gray,
And does the sun get chased away?
Does the sun go to visit the moon?
And will it be returning soon?

A Book For Girls About Being A Girl

ADDING TO THE FAMILY

Do dogs talk to each other?
And does a puppy miss his mother?
Is it the same for a kitty cat,
Or for a mom and baby rat?
I think if I had to leave my mother,
I would try to find another,
Then someone could take me in,
A new life I could begin.
And if I ever lost my mother
Could I also lose my brother?
And then I would feel really bad,
'Cause then I'd also lose my dad.
But some kids just don't have a choice,
And they never have a voice.
We got a new kid and invited him in,
So a new life he could begin.
And now I have a second brother.
I just hope I get no other!

A Book For Girls About Being A Girl

BOYS

Boys can be lots of trouble
If they come in twos
Then that counts double!
And if they come in threes,
Pray to God upon your knees!
Mommy says someday I'll like boys
And give up all my girly toys,
But that won't be for years to come,
And until that time
Boys are just plain dumb!

A Book For Girls About Being A Girl

GOUNG TO THE MALL

I like to go to the mall;
Sometimes I buy a doll!
Sometimes I buy a dress,
Or get a pedicure 'cause my toes are a mess!
Sometimes we get our hair done
And that is really lots of fun!
And if we behave really well,
We get to ride the Carrousel!

A Book For Girls About Being A Girl

MY GARDEN

I have a garden and I planted seeds
But all I seemed to grow was weeds!
I saw weeds here and there
Weeds were growing everywhere!
And so I went and pulled those weeds
And then something grew from those seeds.
Flowers, flowers, everywhere,
Pretty flowers for my hair!

THINGS I HAVE AND THINGS I LIKE

I like pancakes with maple syrup,
I hate it when my brothers burp,
I like to hear my mother sing
And talk about her wedding ring.
I like to hear of days of old
The best stories ever told.
Mom says I am just a kid
And I get things she never did.
She says that things don't mean love,
And that is something from above.
She says that love you just can't buy,
No matter how you try and try.
So some things we have are the same,
Like love and the stars and the gentle rain!
And so for these things I am quite grateful
Because I have a great big plateful!

A Book For Girls About Being A Girl

THE TEACHER'S PET

I like school and I'm the teacher's pet.
I help her a lot and good grades I get.
But sometimes I still get into trouble,
And I have to make up for it on the double.
I don't get into as much trouble as I could,
Because I'm always, most unusually good.
My brother says it's just not fair,
He always gets into his teacher's hair,
And then he just acts really bad,
And makes my mother very sad.
Dad says he only wants attention,
But then he ends up in detention.
Since I'm the girl, the perfect one,
I get to play and have some fun!

A Book For Girls About Being A Girl

TEARS

**Sometimes I cry alligator tears
Right down my face.
I do it when I act badly
And when I feel disgrace.
My brother doesn't like to cry,
And I've always wondered why,
Because I'll make to you a big confession
Tears show you have learned your lesson!
And then the punishment isn't so bad
And for this I'm really glad.
And so you see girls are so smart
Because making tears is quite an art!**

A Book For Girls About Being A Girl

MY CAT

I like to sleep with my cat
Right beside me in my bed.

I like him on my pillow
Next to my little head.

I like the sound of his little purr,
I like the feel of his soft orange fur.

I like it when he follows me around,
With his little meow sound.

I like his head and his little feet,
I love my kitty because he's sweet!

A Book For Girls About Being A Girl

MY DOG

I had the best dog----
She went to heaven and I miss her a lot
Mom says anyone can leave us any time
So appreciate what you've got.
This is a big thing for me to understand,
Walking in the garden on my mother's hand.

A Book For Girls About Being A Girl

THE HOLES IN MY EARS

**My Mom took me to the jewelry store,
In spite of all my fears,
And then the lady at the store
Went and pierced my ears!
It didn't hurt a single bit,
I'm telling you the truth of it!
And now I just put jewels in there
In holes in ears beneath my hair.**

THE GOOD NIGHT

I like fluffy slippers on my feet,
And in my baby blue nightgown
I look oh so sweet.
Mommy say's I'm her lovey dove,
That God sent me from above.
Then she sends me to my room,
And says that she'll be up real soon,
To tuck me into my little bed,
And place a kiss upon my head.
And then she comes and says, "Good night,"
And everything just feels just right!

A Book For Girls About Being A Girl

TEA WITH DOLLY

**Sometimes at night I serve cookies and tea;
It's just pretend, just dolly and me!
I'm really careful when I pour the teapot,
Because dolly just can't drink a lot!
Otherwise she'll be up all night,
And that would be bad and it wouldn't be right,
Because dolly and me we need our rest,
If we want to look our best.**

A Book For Girls About Being A Girl

DUST BUNNIES

There's a family of them under my bed
And to this I swear,
There's a whole family hopping around
And living under there.
Sometimes I tried to crowd them out.
With shoes and other stuff,
But they just keep on hopping about
Until mom's had enough!
Then she goes and gets a broom
And the bunnies leave my room!

A Book For Girls About Being A Girl

RUFFLEY SOCKS

**My socks are cute with ruffles and bows;
They look real nice and cover my toes.
They keep my feet ever so warm,
Even through a winter storm.
But in summer then off go the socks,
As I flip flop over sand and rocks.
And I know they're over there
Sleeping with my underwear.**

A Book For Girls About Being A Girl

BOYS STINK

I think boys stink
Because they never take a bath
Well maybe sometimes they actually do
Because of mother's wrath!

All they do is run around
They boy sweat, then they smell,
And if cleanliness is next to Godliness
They'll surely go to H_ll!

And so I say go get some soap
And wash your body clean,
Especially your dirty feet
Around your toes and in between.

And don't forget to take a cloth
And wash behind your ears, you know,
Or you'll soon find potatoes there
And they will only grow and grow.

And then your head will just turn green
Behind your ears and in between!
And you'll become a potato head
And never, ever fit in bed.

A Book For Girls About Being A Girl

PETER PAN

I want to be like Peter Pan
So no one will know how old I am,
I want to fly up so high
With Tinkerbell in the sky.
I want to go to Neverland
Where things are sweet and oh so grand
But I will miss my family there,
And about them I really care.
And so I think that I'll stay home
And never ever fly or roam.

A Book For Girls About Being A Girl

ABOUT MONEY

If I had a nickel
I'd by a pickle
But if I had a dime,
Then I'd buy a rhyme.
If I had a dollar,
Then I'd just holler
"Hip, Hip Hooray!
I'll have ice-cream today!"

A Book For Girls About Being A Girl

MY MOM SAYS

**My mom says she wants to be a kid again,
That was the best time of her life,
But the only thing I want to be
Is a mother and a wife!**

BEES

Once there was a little bee
That came up and sat right next to me
I didn't run or scream with fear
But I was worried,
Yes, Oh Dear!

I saw him take his stinger out
But I didn't scream or shout,
And then the bee just flew away
Because he would die,
But not today!

The little bee had work to do
Making honey just for you,
When a bee stings, his life is over,
There's no more flying over clover!

A Book For Girls About Being A Girl

THE END

**This is the end of my little book,
I'm so glad you took a look.
This book is for you and not your brother,
So just tell him to get another!**